Big Shiny Moon!
What's in a Spaceship Space for Kids

Children's Aeronautics & Astronautics Books

BABY PROFESSOR

EDUCATION KIDS

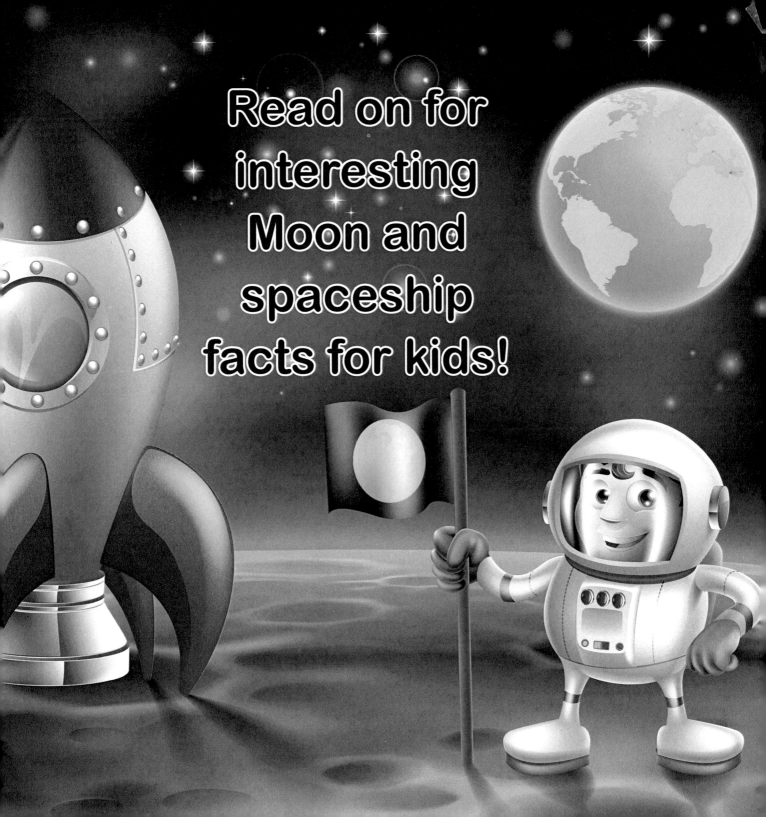

Read on for interesting Moon and spaceship facts for kids!

The Moon is approximately 4.5 billion years old.

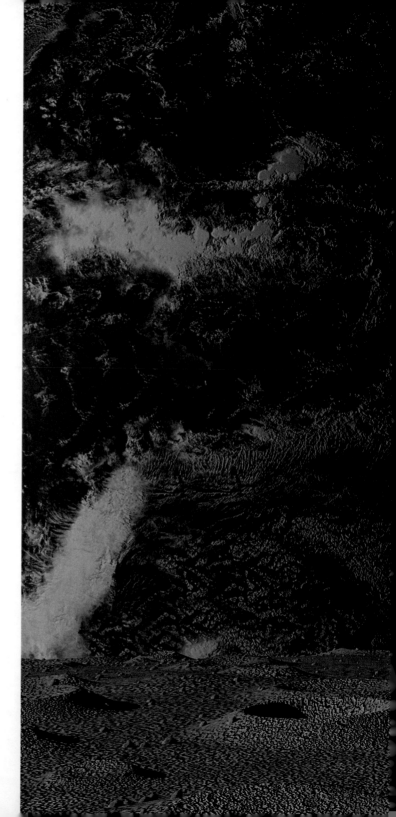

It is the
only natural
satellite in the
Solar System.

You can see the surface of the Moon using binoculars or a small telescope.

The Moon's surface shows the damage caused by rocks hitting it.

The first man
to draw a
proper map
of the Moon
was Galileo.

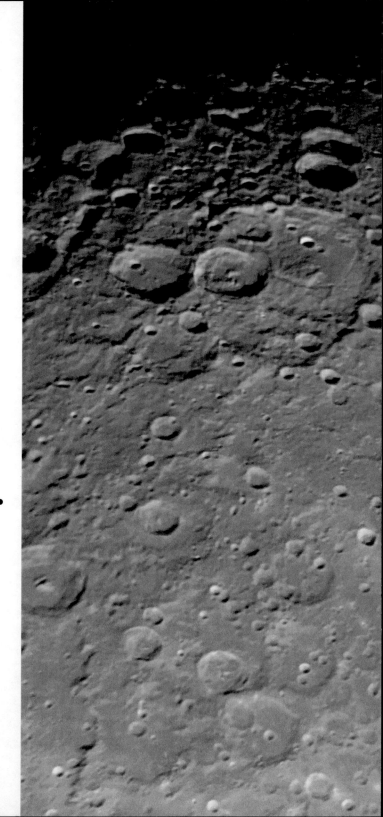

In 1959, Luna 1 was the first spacecraft to reach the Moon.

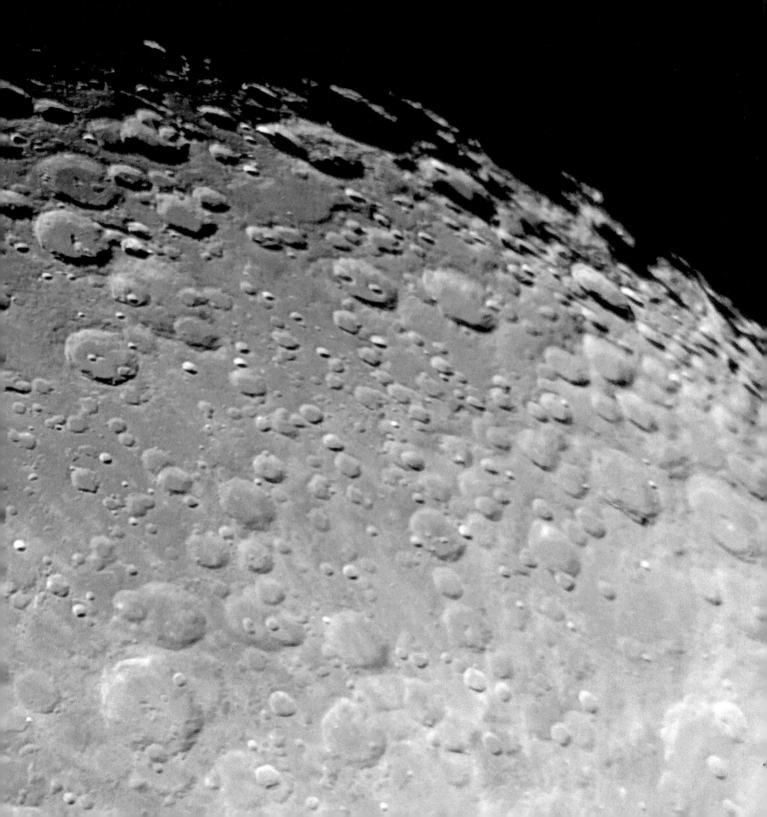

Neil Armstrong
was the first
person to land
on the Moon.

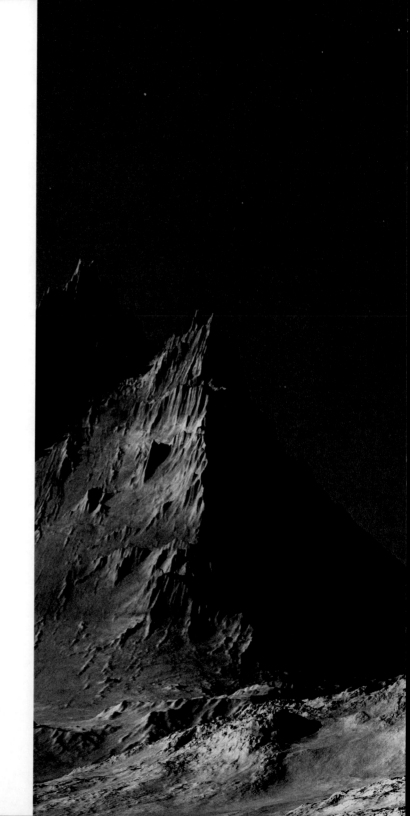

The distance from the Moon to the Earth is 250,000 miles.

Holes in
the Moon
are called
CRATERS.

The Moon orbits the Earth every 27.3 days.

Mons Huygens is the tallest mountain on the Moon, just over half of Mt Everest's height.

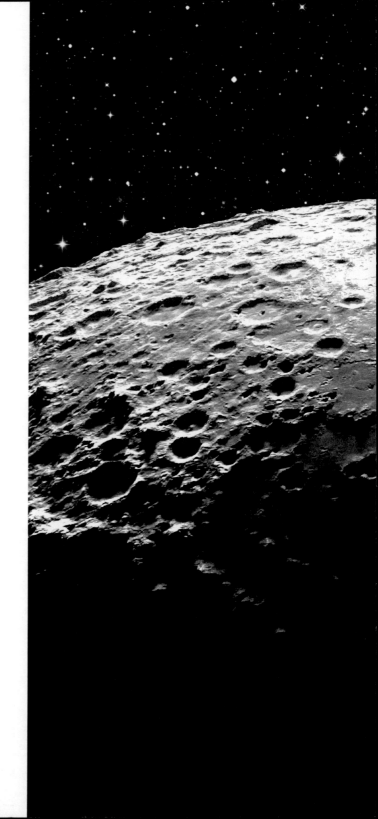

The side we
see is called
the near side
of the Moon
while the other
side is called
the far side.

The Moon is very cold at night but very hot during the day.

The Earth's
tides are
caused by the
gravitational
pull of the
Moon.

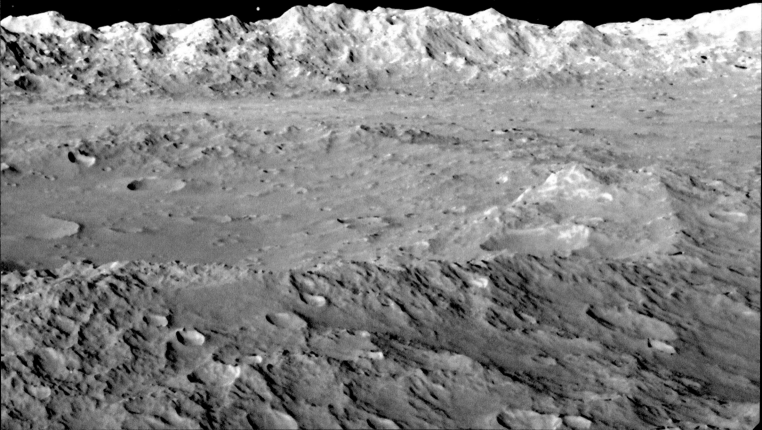

The NASA Apollo 11 mission launched from the USA was the first manned Moon landing (1969).

Earth's gravity is much stronger than the Moons.

The Moon is said to be moving away from earth at about 3.8 cm every year.

Research
and learn
more about
the Moon!
Have fun!

Visit

BABY PROFESSOR
EDUCATION KIDS

www.BabyProfessorBooks.com

to download Free Baby Professor eBooks
and view our catalog of new and exciting
Children's Books

Made in the USA
Middletown, DE
13 June 2017